The Life and Times of

HERNANDO CORTÉS

Mitchell Lane
PUBLISHERS

P.O. Box 196 · Hockessin, Delaware 19707

Titles in the Series

The Life and Times of

HERNANDO CORTÉS

Jim Whiting

Printing   1   2   3   4   5   6   7   8   9

Library of Congress Cataloging-in-Publication Data
Whiting Jim, 1943–.
    The life and times of Hernando Cortés / by Jim Whiting.
        p. cm. — (Profiles in American history)
    Includes bibliographical references and index.
    ISBN 1-58415-449-7 (library bound : alk. paper)
    1. Cortés, Hernán, 1485–1547—Juvenile literature. 2. Conquerors—Mexico—Biography—Juvenile literature. 3. Explorers—Mexico—Biography—Juvenile literature. 4. Explorers—Spain—Biography—Juvenile literature. 5. Mexico—History—Conquest, 1519–1540—Juvenile literature. 6. America—Discovery and exploration—Spanish—Juvenile literature. I. Title. II. Series.
F1230.C835W48 2006
972'.02092—dc22   2005028497

ISBN-10: 1-58415-449-7   ISBN-13: 9781584154495

ABOUT THE AUTHOR: Jim Whiting has been a remarkably versatile and accomplished journalist, writer, editor, and photographer for more than 30 years. A voracious reader since early childhood, Mr. Whiting has written and edited about 200 nonfiction children's books. His subjects range from authors to zoologists and include contemporary pop icons and classical musicians, saints and scientists, emperors and explorers. Representative titles include *The Life and Times of Franz Liszt*, *The Life and Times of Julius Caesar*, *Charles Schulz*, *Charles Darwin and the Origin of the Species*, *Juan Ponce de Leon*, and *The Life and Times of John Adams*.

    He lives in Washington State with his wife and two teenage sons.

PHOTO CREDITS: Cover, pp. 6, 20, 36—North Wind Picture Archives; p. 28—Hulton Archive/Getty Images; pp. 1, 3, 12—Library of Congress; pp. 10, 16, 40—Barbara Marvis; pp. 9, 14, 26—Sharon Beck.

PUBLISHER'S NOTE: This story is based on the author's extensive research, which he believes to be accurate. Documentation of such research is contained on page 46.

    The internet sites referenced herein were active as of the publication date. Due to the fleeting nature of some web sites, we cannot guarantee they will all be active when you are reading this book.

PLB

Contents

*For Your Information

Aztec Emperor Montezuma (left) greets Spanish leader Cortés at the entrance to his palace in November 1519. He gave Cortés gold and other valuable gifts, hoping the Spanish would move past Tenochtitlán and out of the Aztec Empire. He was wrong. The gifts only made the Spanish greedy for more.

CHAPTER
1

The Night of Sorrows

The escape began at midnight. The men were almost out of food and fresh water. Many suffered from painful wounds. They were trapped in the heart of Tenochtitlán, the capital city of the Aztec Empire. The Aztecs were also known as Mexicans. Their city was located on an island in a huge lake. Narrow causeways a few feet above the water were the only link to the mainland—and safety.

The men had marched into the city on November 9, 1519. When they arrived, they were honored guests. Montezuma II, the Aztec leader, believed the men might be gods. He gave them a fortune in gold and many other valuable objects.

The visitors weren't gods. They were Spanish soldiers, commanded by Hernando Cortés. Although they had received a friendly welcome, Cortés didn't want to take any chances. He took Montezuma as a hostage. That had protected them for more than six months—until Cortés had to leave for several weeks. While he was gone, his men slaughtered thousands of defenseless Aztecs during a festival. In retaliation, the Aztecs attacked the soldiers.

Even after Cortés returned, the attacks continued. The Aztecs cut off the heads of the Spaniards they killed, mounted the heads on sticks, then waved these "trophies" in front of the defenders. Some Spaniards had been captured. Their fate was even worse. The Aztecs believed in human sacrifice. They sliced open the

chests of their prisoners and ripped out their hearts. The victims were still alive during this gruesome process.

In desperation, Cortés brought Montezuma out on a rooftop. The ruler ordered his people to stop attacking the Spanish, but it was too late. The Aztecs no longer respected him. Many threw stones at him, and he was injured badly. Montezuma died a few days later.

Cortés knew he had to try to get out of the city. He and about 1,300 Spanish soldiers, plus about 2,000 Indians from the town of Tlaxcala, were surrounded by tens of thousands of Aztecs. Soon the Aztecs would overwhelm them.

His only hope was to try to sneak out at night while the Aztecs were asleep. He had to make his attempt in complete silence. He whispered orders to his different commanders, and the commanders whispered the orders to their men. One of the orders was to wrap cloth around the hooves of their horses to muffle the sound of their retreat.

Cortés knew there were gaps in the causeways. The Aztecs had removed bridges that joined each section. The water between each section was too deep to wade through. The Spanish built a portable bridge that they could lay across each gap.

Besides the portable bridge, the men carried hundreds of pounds of gold. Of the treasures they had amassed, Cortés claimed one portion for himself and another for the king of Spain. He gave the rest to his men. They all became very wealthy.

This sudden wealth had a downside. Gold is heavy. If a man took his full share, he would be weighed down, making it hard to fight. If he took only a little, it would be much easier to fight, but he wouldn't be very wealthy.

A light rain began to fall shortly before the men began moving out. The long column proceeded across the causeway. Three times they came to a gap. Each time they laid down the portable bridge. Slowly, silently, the men crossed the water. Many began to believe they would make it.

Then an Aztec woman who had gone outside to get some water saw them. "Our enemies are leaving!" she screamed. "Now that it is night they are running away."[1]

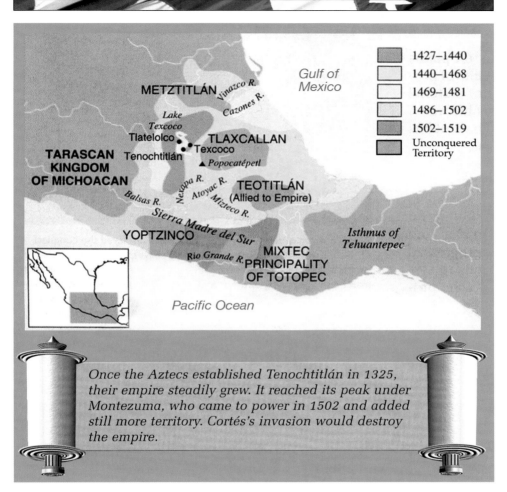

Once the Aztecs established Tenochtitlán in 1325, their empire steadily grew. It reached its peak under Montezuma, who came to power in 1502 and added still more territory. Cortés's invasion would destroy the empire.

Within minutes hundreds of canoes, filled with angry Aztec warriors, swarmed around the Spanish. The fighting was brutal. Some of the Spanish panicked. In their haste to escape, they threw away the portable bridge. When they came to another gap in the causeway, there was no alternative but to plunge into the water. "The canal was soon choked with the bodies of men and horses; they filled the gap in the causeway with their own drowned bodies," an Aztec account explained. "Those who followed crossed to the other side by walking on the corpses."[2]

The Aztecs especially wanted to capture Cortés—by now they knew he wasn't a god. He and the other Spaniards were men, just

The famous Mexican painter Diego Rivera depicts Tenochtitlán at the height of its power. The city was much larger than most European cities of the same era. Its people enjoyed a high standard of living.

like they were. Twice they nearly took him prisoner. Both times Cortés's men were able to pull him to safety.

Somehow, Cortés and about 400 other Spanish managed to survive. Nearly 900 didn't. The men at the rear of the column weren't as lucky. They were clubbed to death, drowned, or captured for immediate sacrifice. Many of the Tlaxcala perished as well.

The Spanish called the event *La Noche Triste* (Night of Sorrows). It was their first major military disaster in the New World.

Cortés, who was normally very optimistic, wept when he realized how badly he had been defeated. It was probably the lowest point of his life.

In just over a year, the situation would be completely reversed. Tenochtitlán would lie in ruins at Cortés's feet. He would be the master of the Aztec Empire.

The Aztecs

The Aztecs were not the first group of people to occupy the site of Tenochtitlán. There is evidence that a civilization existed there early in the first century CE—around the time Jesus of Nazareth was born. This civilization was replaced a few hundred years later by the Toltecs. They too lost power. Their legendary hero Quetzalcoatl left the city but promised to return.

The Aztecs arrived in the thirteenth century from a mythical homeland called Aztlán. To honor one of their early leaders, Mexitli, they called themselves Mexica. They founded Tenochtitlán in 1325. Their power grew rapidly. First they overcame tribes that bordered on Lake Texcoco, where Tenochtitlán was located. Then they moved farther away from the lake. At its height, the empire stretched from the Pacific Ocean to the Atlantic, from the middle of modern-day Mexico south to Guatemala.

Their pride was reflected in the capital. Tenochtitlán had begun as a swamp. The Aztecs began filling it in with dirt and rocks until it was an island in the shape of a square. Each side measured two miles. Many canals crisscrossed the city, and these divided it into numerous smaller neighborhoods. The canals also helped to control flooding, which was a constant danger. The island was only a few feet above the surface of the lake.

The Aztecs could boast of many achievements. They constructed thousands of buildings. Some, such as the temples, were especially magnificent. They built a pipeline from the mainland to ensure a steady supply of fresh water. The marketplace was far larger than anything in Europe at that time. There were many beautiful gardens.

The Aztecs believed in a number of gods. The most important was Huitzilopochtli (left), the god of the sun. The main temple in the city was dedicated to him. The Aztecs believed that Huitzilopochtli demanded a steady stream of blood. Without it, he would die—and the sun wouldn't rise. They obtained some of their victims in battle. Others came from the cities they had already conquered. These cities were required to send a certain number of their people at regular intervals for sacrifice. The Aztecs believed their victims should feel honored. It was a privilege to be sacrificed, they felt, because their deaths contributed to the survival of the people of Tenochtitlán.

11

Hernando Cortés was painted by the Master of Saldana, who showed the conqueror at the peak of his power. The portrait hangs in the National Museum of History in Mexico City.

CHAPTER 2

A Nobody Becomes a Somebody

Hernando Cortés was born in 1485 in Medellín, a city in the province of Extremadura, Spain. His father was Martín Cortés de Monroy, a minor nobleman who owned a few acres of land. He was also an experienced military man. Hernando's mother was Doña Catalina Pizarro Altamirano de Cortés.

In an era of large families, Hernando was unusual. He was an only child. As a baby, he was very sickly. His nurse often lighted candles for his survival on the church altar.

He was born into a violent era. More than 700 years earlier, Islamic Moors from North Africa had conquered Catholic Spain. Within a few years, the Spanish slowly began reclaiming their territory. For centuries, the countryside was ravaged by war between the two religions. Early in 1492, the Moors were expelled from the city of Granada, their last outpost in Spain. Later that year, Christopher Columbus set out on his historic expedition. He discovered the New World.

By that time, Hernando had become much healthier. He enjoyed many outdoor activities. Often he and the other children played warlike games such as Christians and Moors. It was similar to modern-day cops and robbers. They also probably played an early version of soccer. The prayers of his nurse had seemingly been answered.

Cortés was born in Medellín, Spain, near the border with Portugal. Seville, which would be an important city for Cortés in his later years, was an inland port. It was connected to the Mediterranean Sea by the Guadalquivir River.

Going to church had a major influence on Hernando's life. He grew up firmly believing Christianity was the true religion. His countrymen felt the same way. They believed that God had helped them overthrow the Moors. They took their religious attitudes with them to the New World. They believed that their divine mission was to convert the people they found to Christianity.

When Hernando was fourteen, his father sent him to the University of Salamanca. Martín wanted his son to become a lawyer. He knew that the law would provide a steady source of income. That was especially important in Extremadura, where the land was harsh and bleak. It was hard to grow crops, and besides farming, there weren't many other ways of earning money.

Hernando dropped out of the university after just two years. No one knows why. He was apparently a good student. His parents were disappointed in his decision, but they believed there was a good alternate plan for him.

At that time, a trickle of gold was starting to come back to Spain from the New World. Many Spaniards believed there was a great deal more just waiting to be discovered. Some of them were men who had fought the Moors. With no more battles to fight, they were bored. They wanted to do something exciting. Teenagers who listened to their war stories were also looking for adventure. Going to the New World offered the opportunity for both excitement and great riches.

Hernando's parents knew a man named Nicolás de Ovando, who had just been appointed governor of the island of Hispaniola. Columbus had discovered the island a decade earlier. Many Spaniards were going there, and Ovando agreed to take the boy with him.

Hernando didn't make the trip. Now seventeen, he was having a love affair with a married woman. Her husband found out. As Hernando was trying to escape, he fell and was badly injured. Ovando's ships left without him.

Hernando recovered slowly. To pass the time, he read a lot. In that era, adventure-filled romance stories had just become popular. The most famous was *Amadís of Gaul*. It was a bestseller on the scale of the modern-day Harry Potter books. A sequel to *Amadís of Gaul*, called *Adventures of Esplandián*, influenced Hernando's later life. The book became very important for the future United States of America.

Eventually Hernando's injuries healed. He drifted aimlessly for about a year. His wanderings took him to some of Spain's port cities, where he met men who had just returned from the New World. After hearing their stories, he decided to go there himself. He was eighteen when he boarded a ship in 1503. There was nothing special about him.

The voyage across the Atlantic Ocean was not pleasant. His ship nearly sank in a storm, and then it ran out of food and water.

The University of Salamanca, where Cortés studied for two years, was founded in 1218. The school is still in existence and has more than 30,000 students.

When he finally arrived, Ovando gave him a little land, and Hernando settled on Hispaniola. For nearly a decade, he did nothing that stood out. He was just one of hundreds of young Spaniards trying to make his fortune, using slave labor of the native peoples to work the mines. There was one difference. Cortés served under an important man named Don Diego Velázquez. In 1511, Velázquez received permission to conquer the island of Cuba, where he would serve as governor. Cortés went with him.

For several years, all went well for Cortés. Many Spaniards wanted to get rich quick, but Cortés was a little different. He liked to plan for the future. He didn't overwork his slaves. He mined slowly and cautiously. He practiced farming as scientifically as he could, given the limited knowledge of his era. Velázquez appointed him mayor of the town of Santiago. He became reasonably wealthy and married Catalina Suarez. He might have continued in this way for the rest of his life.

Velázquez, who heard rumors regarding a rich land west of Cuba, organized an expedition in 1517. It landed in the Yucatán Peninsula of modern-day Mexico. The native peoples on Cuba and Hispaniola hadn't put up much of a fight. The people on the Yucatán were very different. Making it clear that they didn't want the Spaniards on their land, they killed many of the invaders. The survivors managed to bring back some gold. They learned it had come from the Aztecs, who lived farther north in a land called Mexico.

Velázquez was much more interested in the gold than in the dead men. He sent another expedition the following year. It returned with even more gold.

He decided to send a third expedition later in 1518. He wasn't sure whom to appoint as the leader. Some men turned him down. Others were willing, but he didn't trust them. Behind Velázquez's back, Cortés made a deal with two leading merchants, asking them to suggest him to Velázquez. If they did, he would share the profits with them when he returned.

Many people were surprised when Velázquez chose Hernando. Cortés had never shown any abilities as a leader. Almost overnight he seemed to change his personality. He dressed better. He appeared to be more responsible. He even hired bodyguards. It was almost as if he had suddenly grown up.

One thing hadn't changed. From the time he was young, he had never opened up about his feelings. As historian Jon Manchip White notes, "His complete control of his emotions, under every condition of stress and provocation, was largely responsible for his success."[1]

One of his first acts was to make a banner that showed how important Christianity was to him. It read: "Brothers and comrades, in true faith let us follow the Holy Cross and we shall conquer."[2]

He spent nearly all his money to organize the expedition. He borrowed even more. He hired three hundred men, all experienced in battle. Even more important, he was able to acquire fifty horses. No one in the New World was familiar with horses. Mounted men seemed like giants to the natives.

"These 'stags,' these 'horses,' snort and bellow," wrote one of the Aztecs. "They sweat a great deal, the sweat pours from their

The Spanish mastiff weighs well over 200 pounds. It has been used as a guardian for both sheep and cattle. Cortés used these dogs to attack native people in Mexico.

bodies in streams. The foam from their muzzles drips onto the ground. It spills out in fat drops. . . . They make a loud noise when they run; they make a great din, as if stones were raining on the earth."[3]

Besides horses, Cortés brought many mastiffs—huge dogs with ferocious tempers. At a word of command, they would rush at the natives and attack them viciously. Often the victims would die.

He took advantage of the best of European killing technology. He had several cannons. Many of his men were armed with harquebuses, an early version of the rifle. Many more carried crossbows. Almost all wore heavy armor.

Velázquez became uneasy about the expedition. He had never really trusted Cortés, and many people didn't like him. They spread nasty rumors about him to Velázquez. Even though the rumors weren't true, the governor decided to cancel the deal.

Cortés quickly learned of Velázquez's decision. He knew it was likely he would be arrested. He rushed through final preparations. Velázquez tried to prevent Cortés from leaving, but Cortés defied him. He set sail for Mexico.

It was February 1519, and Hernando Cortés was about to change the course of history.

The Maya

A Mayan temple

The Mayan civilization goes back about 3,000 years. It became important just before the birth of Jesus of Nazareth and reached its peak about a thousand years later. The Maya didn't have a central government. Instead, they developed a number of city-states. People from all the city-states spoke a similar language and held similar cultural beliefs.

Most of their economy was based on growing crops. Chocolate was one of the best-known products. Historians believe that the word *chocolate* comes from the Mayan word *xocolatl* (pronounced *shah-koh-LAA-tul*). The Maya had large farms to grow cacao beans. The beans were used as currency and to produce chocolate and cocoa. Some marriage ceremonies ended with the bride and groom drinking cocoa together.

The Maya were scientifically and culturally accomplished. They were very good at mathematics and had developed extremely accurate calendars. Their art and their literature were well developed. Catholic priests who arrived in the sixteenth century destroyed most of the books the Maya wrote.

The best-known Mayan settlement was at Chichén Itzá. Today, its ruins are a popular tourist site. Visitors can climb to the tops of several large temples, look at sculptures and down deep wells, and see a large court where the Maya used to play a ferocious ballgame.

The court is huge. Three football fields could fit inside its walls. The object was for one team to knock the ball—probably the size of a soccer ball—into the other end of the court. Sometimes the teams had to put the ball through a stone ring. The game was very violent. Most players wore thick padding, but injuries and even death were considered part of the game. Occasionally the losing team would be put to death.

The arrival of the Spanish ended the independent Mayan civilization. Unlike many other conquered civilizations, the Maya still survive. Millions of Maya live in Mexico, Guatemala, and Belize. Many speak languages based on Nahuatl, their native tongue.

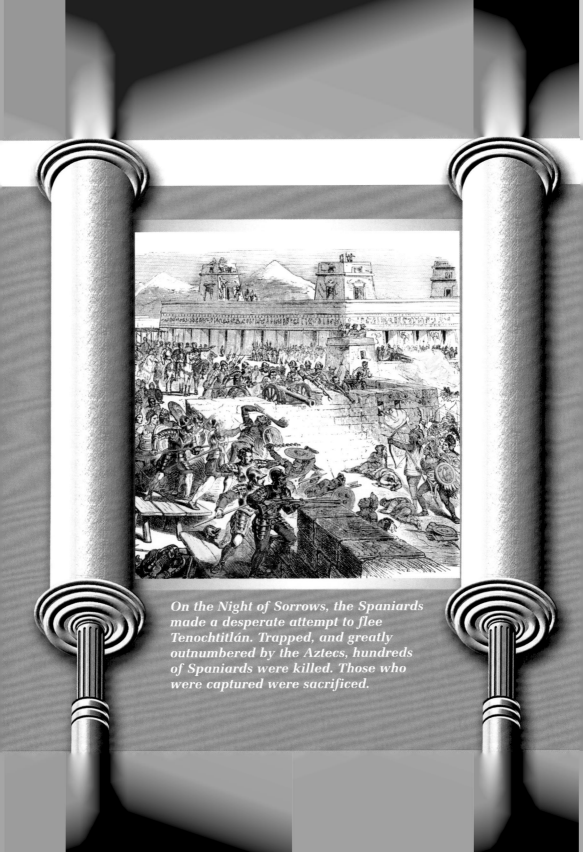

On the Night of Sorrows, the Spaniards made a desperate attempt to flee Tenochtitlán. Trapped, and greatly outnumbered by the Aztecs, hundreds of Spaniards were killed. Those who were captured were sacrificed.

CHAPTER
3

The Halls of Montezuma

What happened next is well documented. Cortés sent long letters describing his experiences to the Spanish king, Charles I. Several men on the expedition, notably Bernal Díaz del Castillo, wrote long, detailed accounts. The Aztecs also wrote stories concerning this time.

Cortés's first landfall was Cozumel, an island a few miles off the eastern shore of the Yucatán Peninsula. There he had a stroke of luck. He found a Spanish priest named Jerónimo de Aguilar. Aguilar was a shipwreck victim who had been enslaved by the Maya. He had learned the language of his captors. He joined Cortés. Now Cortés could communicate with the Maya.

Then Cortés got even luckier. After winning a battle, he was given a woman named Malintzin. He gave her the Spanish name of Doña Marina. She spoke both Mayan and Nahuatl, the language of the Aztecs. Now he could carry on very detailed conversations with anyone he met. Marina would translate Nahuatl into Mayan for Aguilar. Aguilar would translate into Spanish for Cortés. Marina eventually learned Spanish, which made her even more valuable. She also became very important to Cortés on a personal level.

Her reputation among modern-day Mexicans is very different. She inspired the word *malinchista*. The word is a term of contempt

for a person who prefers foreigners to Mexicans. It means the person isn't trustworthy.

As Cortés sailed west along the Yucatán coast, he learned that the Aztecs controlled many of the local Indian tribes. The tribes weren't happy with that situation. Some even openly resisted the Aztecs. Cortés would use this knowledge to devastating effect.

In late April, he anchored off the eastern coast of Mexico and founded a settlement named Villa Rica de la Vera Cruz. Today it is the city of Veracruz. It is one of Mexico's most important ports.

The Aztecs knew where he was. A system of relay runners brought word to Montezuma. The runners described fearsome fair-skinned strangers with beards. The men on horseback were especially frightening.

Montezuma might have destroyed Cortés and his handful of men if he had acted immediately. The Spaniards weren't familiar with the country. Montezuma could have sent thousands of warriors against them.

Montezuma hesitated. According to the Aztec religion, the new arrivals may have marked the return of Quetzalcoatl, the legendary ruler. He had always promised to return. Because he was related to the sun, and the sun rose in the east, it made sense that he would return from the east. Cortés had landed on the east coast of Mexico. Like Quetzalcoatl, he had a beard and light skin.

For nearly ten years before Cortés arrived, a series of unusual events had occurred. Comets streaked across the sky in broad daylight. The mysterious voice of a wailing woman awoke people in the middle of the night. A column of fire appeared in the eastern sky for months on end. Aztec priests believed these and other omens indicated that Quetzalcoatl was about to come back.

There was still another coincidence. Quetzalcoatl had been born in the year Ce Acatl in the Aztec calendar. His return would take place in the same year. By coincidence, 1519 happened to be another Ce Acatl. Montezuma didn't want to take any chances by killing a god.

Instead of his army, Montezuma sent an emissary. The emissary told Cortés not to come to Tenochtitlán. The passage was hard and difficult, he warned. He also brought gifts of gold from Montezuma.

Montezuma hoped the gifts would be enough to make the Spaniards leave his country. He didn't know that the Spanish were very greedy for gold. His gifts made Cortés even more eager to meet Montezuma. There must be much more gold in Tenochtitlán, he believed.

Not all of his men supported Cortés. Some wanted to sail back to Cuba. Cortés hanged their leader. Then he stripped the ships of everything useful and sank them. He stored what he had saved in Vera Cruz. He and his men could only go forward.

They set off on a march of more than 200 miles, most of it through mountainous terrain. That wasn't the only difficulty. An Indian tribe called the Tlaxcalans didn't want Cortés to pass through their territory. They thought Cortés might support the Aztecs, whom they hated. The two sides met in battle. The Spaniards suffered some losses; the Tlaxcalans lost many more men. Realizing they couldn't defeat the Spaniards, they asked for peace. Far more important, they agreed to join Cortés on his journey.

The Tlaxcalans warned him about the next city on his route, Cholula. They said the Cholulans would attack the Spaniards. Cortés got the jump on his would-be enemies. He invited the city's leaders to a banquet—and then he killed them.

Montezuma sent more emissaries to Cortés. They gave him even more gold. The emissaries were amused by the reaction of these foreigners. One of them reported, "When they were given these presents, the Spaniards burst into smiles; their eyes shone with pleasure; they were delighted by them. They picked up the gold and fingered it like monkeys. . . . They longed and lusted for gold. Their bodies swelled with greed, and their hunger was ravenous; they hungered like pigs for that gold."[1]

Soon the Spaniards sighted Tenochtitlán, which was also called Mexico. They could barely believe what they saw. "And when we saw so many cities and villages built in the water and other great towns on dry land and that straight and narrow Causeway going towards Mexico we were amazed," wrote Díaz del Castillo. "The great towns and cues [temples] and buildings rising from the water, all made of masonry, [and it] seemed like an enchanted vision. And some of our soldiers even asked whether the things we saw were not a dream."[2]

It is no wonder that the men thought they might be dreaming. Most had come from small towns back home. They were dirt-poor. Nothing in their lives prepared them for such magnificence. When they marched into the city, it was an act of supreme confidence. There were less than 400 of them. Even with the Tlaxcalans, they were greatly outnumbered.

Montezuma invited the Spaniards to stay at his palace. He staged elaborate banquets and gave his visitors guided tours of the splendor of his city.

Cortés wasn't a fool. He knew he had put himself and his men in danger. Eight days after arriving, he made a daring move. Cortés put Montezuma under arrest, holding the Aztec leader hostage. Cortés wanted to use Montezuma as a mouthpiece for his own orders.

One of his first orders was to see Montezuma's treasure. His men couldn't believe their good fortune. The Aztecs relate: "The Spaniards grinned like little beasts and patted each other with delight. When they entered the hall of treasures, it was as if they had arrived in Paradise."[3]

Cortés knew he wasn't in Paradise. He couldn't hold Montezuma forever, and tensions were building. Differences in religious practice were one source of tension. Cortés was appalled by the Aztecs' rite of human sacrifice. The priests horrified him. They never bathed. Their hair was caked with dried blood. Often they would wear the skin of their victims. It was common for them to roast human body parts and eat them.

Cortés wanted the Aztecs to become Christians. He tried to put Christian symbols on their religious pyramids. He tried to destroy the Aztec religion.

This unstable peace lasted about six months. Then Cortés got some shattering news. In April 1520, Velázquez sent his trusted lieutenant, Pánfilo de Narváez, to bring back Cortés. Narváez landed in Mexico with 900 men.

Cortés acted swiftly. He immediately marched for the coast with about 300 men. He left Pedro de Alvarado in command of the other 120.

Cortés didn't want to fight his fellow Spaniards. Historians believe that he secretly sent a message to Narváez's men to let them

know that they were welcome to join him. If they did, he assured them that they would become rich themselves.

Cortés attacked during a driving rainstorm. Narváez hadn't posted guards, because he didn't believe that Cortés would attack him in such bad weather. Hardly anyone was killed during the short battle. Narváez lost one eye and was captured. Almost all of his men agreed to join Cortés. He had more than tripled the size of his army. It appeared that his luck was still holding.

It wasn't. Díaz del Castillo wrote, "Let me say how ill luck suddenly turns the wheel, and after great good fortune and pleasure follows sadness; it so happened that at this moment came the news that Pedro de Alvarado was besieged in his fortress and quarters, and that they had set fire to this same fortress in two places, and had killed seven of his soldiers and wounded many others, and he sent to demand assistance with great urgency and haste."[4]

Cortés returned to a scene of chaos. Alvarado had not governed well. The Aztecs had careful rules to regulate violence, and the Spanish had violated all of them. Worst of all, he had attacked during one of the Aztecs' most important festivals. Spanish soldiers slaughtered thousands of unarmed people. According to an Aztec account,

> [The Spaniards] ran in among the dancers, forcing their way to the place where the drums were played. They attacked the man who was drumming and cut off his arms. Then they cut off his head, and it rolled across the floor. They attacked all the celebrants, stabbing them, spearing them, striking them with their swords. They attacked some of them from behind, and these fell instantly to the ground with their entrails [stomach and intestines] hanging out. Others they beheaded; they cut off their heads, or split their heads to pieces.[5]

The Aztecs were furious. They allowed Cortés and his expanded army to return, and then they resumed the siege. Cortés hoped Montezuma could calm his people. Instead, the Aztecs threw stones at him. When Montezuma died, Cortés was forced to plan his desperate escape.

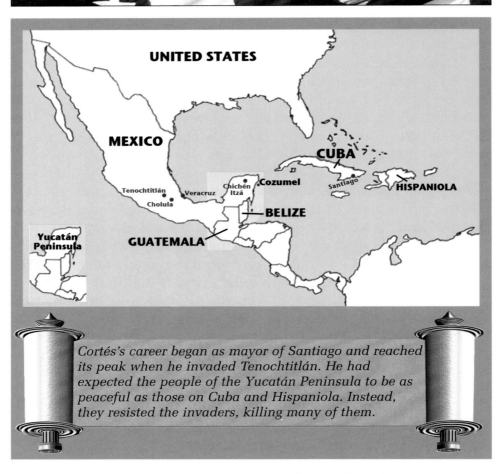

Cortés's career began as mayor of Santiago and reached its peak when he invaded Tenochtitlán. He had expected the people of the Yucatán Peninsula to be as peaceful as those on Cuba and Hispaniola. Instead, they resisted the invaders, killing many of them.

Almost all the men who died on the Night of Sorrows were from Narváez's army. Cortés had promised them wealth. He was as good as his word—but they had had less than a week to enjoy it.

While the Aztecs were killing hundreds of his men, Cortés reached temporary safety. For one of the few times in his life, he showed emotion. He broke down and cried.

His breakdown didn't last long. Soon he became optimistic. Most of the men in the original group that had landed with him had survived. They included his best commanders and Doña Marina.

Even as Cortés fled from Tenochtitlán, he was forming a plan for returning. Hernando Cortés wasn't about to give up.

The Narváez Expedition to Florida

Pánfilo Narváez must have been a very persuasive man. He failed to capture Cortés, lost an eye, and spent two years in prison. Yet he convinced King Charles I to give him command of an expedition to Florida. Many Spanish believed that Florida contained large amounts of gold.

Florida had been discovered in 1513 by Juan Ponce de León. Eight years later, Ponce de León tried to start a colony there. He was seriously wounded by a native Floridian's arrow and died soon afterward. The expedition was a failure.

Narváez landed in Florida in 1528 with several ships and 400 men. When he landed, a native chief met him. Narváez asked the chief where he could find gold. The chief didn't know. Narváez cut off the man's nose. The chief pointed to the north. He knew there wasn't any gold—he just wanted to get rid of Narváez.

Narváez split his forces, which proved to be a mistake. He would march north with most of his men. He told the rest of his men to sail to a port in Mexico called Pánuco, and he would meet them there. He thought the port was about 100 miles away. The actual distance was 1,500 miles. The ships sailed away and never saw Narváez again.

Panfilo Narváez in Florida

Narváez trekked north through Florida. It was very hot. The swamps were hard to get through, and none of the natives wanted to help him. There was no gold. There was also very little food.

In desperation, Narváez built some large canoes. He planned to sail along the coast of the Gulf of Mexico to Pánuco. Along the way, some of the canoes vanished, including Narváez's. Others made it to shore. Many of the men soon died. One of the few survivors, Álvar Núñez Cabeza de Vaca, lived for several years among the Indians in Texas. Then he made a 2,000-mile trek to Mexico City. When he arrived, he was hailed as a hero. He inspired the governor to send Francisco Vásquez de Coronado on an expedition to find gold. Coronado explored the American southwest for two years. Like Narváez, he didn't find any gold.

After his narrow escape from Tenochtitlán, Cortés rallied his forces. He defeated the Aztecs at the Battle of Otumba. Shortly after the battle, he entered Tlaxcala, the city of his Indian allies.

CHAPTER 4

Taking Tenochtitlán

Cortés had to complete his escape. He led his tiny band around the northern end of the lake, then turned east toward the safety of Tlaxcala. At least he hoped it would be safe. He had no idea whether the Tlaxcalans would remain friendly.

The Aztecs were hot on his heels. They caught up with him at the town of Otumba, about halfway to Tlaxcala. More than 40,000 enemies threatened to destroy him and his remaining men.

Cortés called on his most trusted and experienced warriors. They charged on horseback at the Aztec leaders, killing many and capturing their brightly colored banners. Without their leaders, the Aztecs fled. Finally Cortés arrived in Tlaxcala.

By this time, many of his men were very unhappy. "Our heads are broken, our bodies are rotting and covered with wounds and sores, bloodless, weak, and naked," wrote his secretary, Francisco López de Gómara. "We are in a strange land, poor, sick, surrounded by enemies, and without hope of rising from the spot where we fall. We would be fools and idiots if we should let ourselves in for another risk like the past one."[1]

Cortés had to bolster his troops. He knew it would be expensive to carry out his intentions, so, using his powerful, persuasive

personality, he convinced his grumbling men to buy into his plan. He managed to get all their remaining gold. Losing their wealth didn't make his troops feel any better.

It helped that he didn't have to worry about the loyalty of the Tlaxcalans. They had already been impressed with Cortés. He had marched to Tenochtitlán, had gotten into the city, and had captured Montezuma. The Tlaxcalans were even more impressed that he had escaped and killed thousands of enemies. Many other native peoples began joining him as well.

Cortés put them to work. One of his first questions when he recovered from his momentary breakdown was about Martín López, a master boat builder. López had been badly wounded, but he wasn't dead. His survival was one of the few bright spots to come from the Night of Sorrows.

Cortés had learned a bitter lesson that night. It wasn't enough to control the island. He also had to control Lake Texcoco. He put López in charge of a crash program in shipbuilding. Hundreds of men chopped down trees. Hundreds more shaped the trees into planks, ribs, and masts. Still more men went to Vera Cruz to gather the fittings from the ships that Cortés had sunk.

López's task was to build thirteen vessels—not just glorified rowboats, but small ships, with masts and sails. López designed them with high decks to prevent the Aztecs from coming alongside and boarding. The decks were strong enough to support cannons. They also provided protection for men armed with crossbows and harquebuses.

If López built the ships on the edge of the lake, the Aztecs would be able to attack him and destroy the ships. He decided to build them in Tlaxcala, then dismantle them so that they could be carried to the shore.

Back in Tenochtitlán, the Aztecs were optimistic. They were unaware of what was taking place in Tlaxcala. They were happy that they had gotten rid of Cortés. They had quickly replaced Montezuma. The new leader's name was Cuitlahuac, a man who had advised against admitting the Spanish in the first place.

Within a few months, however, Cortés had an invisible ally. Thousands of Aztecs began dying of a mysterious illness. They

were covered with the painful sores of smallpox. According to Díaz del Castillo, the disease had arrived with Narváez and a "man whom he brought covered with smallpox . . . it was owing to him that the whole country was stricken and filled with it, from which there was great mortality, for according to what the Indians said they had never seen such a disease, and, as they did not understand it, they bathed very often, and on that account a great number of them died."[2]

No matter how it arrived, the disease was devastating. The Aztecs had no natural defenses against it. Cuitlahuac was one of the victims.

Cortés had other advantages. No one outside of Mexico knew what was happening with him. He could conceal his defeat from the outside world. He also acquired Spanish reinforcements. Some were from Velázquez, seeking word of Narváez. Others came from Jamaica, seeking to start a colony. Cortés easily convinced the new arrivals to join him. Many had horses and powerful weapons.

In April 1521, Cortés was ready. He led his army back toward Tenochtitlán. Thousands of men carried the dismantled parts of the little ships. When they arrived at the shore of the lake, López supervised the ships' reassembly.

Cortés did not want to resort to outright fighting. He hoped the Aztecs would surrender when they saw how many men and ships he had. According to some estimates, more than 200,000 natives had joined Cortés. The new ruler of Tenochtitlán, Cuauhtémoc, defied Cortés. He executed some of the nobles who wanted to surrender to the Spaniards.

Cortés was right about his little ships. As noted military historian Victor Davis Hanson points out, "[The ships] proved the deciding factor in the entire war, as they were manned by a third of the Spanish manpower and were allotted nearly 75 percent of the cannon, harquebuses, and crossbows. The ships kept the causeways free, ensured that the Spanish camps were secure in the evening, landed infantry at weak points in the enemy lines, enforced a crippling blockade of the city, systematically blew apart hundreds of Aztec canoes, and transported critical food and supplies to the various isolated Spanish contingents."[3]

The Aztecs were trapped inside Tenochtitlán. They didn't have much food. Cortés cut the supply of fresh water. Slowly he tightened the noose around the city. It was a new experience for the Aztecs. They had never tried to starve an entire population to death.

The fighting became especially bitter. The battle line advanced street by street, house by house. Sometimes the Spanish suffered reverses. Once fifteen men were captured and sacrificed. Another time more than fifty men and four horses were taken. All were sacrificed in plain view of their horrified countrymen.

Even so, Cortés was too powerful. The fighting finally ended nearly three months later. Cuauhtémoc tried to negotiate terms for his surviving people. It didn't do much good. Cortés's native allies ran through the city, slaughtering Aztecs. They wanted revenge for all their people who had been sacrificed.

Nearly all of Tenochtitlán had been destroyed. Cortés began rebuilding the city. He renamed it Mexico City and established a new government. He built a large cathedral on top of the great pyramid that had once held the temple of the Aztec sun god. As he saw it, Christianity had triumphed over the Aztec religion.

Now he had to convince King Charles that he was entitled to govern Mexico City. Velázquez objected. He said that since he had been the one to authorize the original expedition, he should be appointed as its governor. Both men sent letters to Charles.

The king agreed with Cortés. In October 1522, Cortés became governor of what was known as New Spain. He was also appointed captain-general and chief judge.

Just over two decades earlier, Cortés had been a law school dropout. Now he had conquered an entire civilization. He was wealthy and honored. For most men, that would have been enough.

It wasn't enough for Hernando Cortés.

The History of Mexico City

Tenochtitlán was in ruins after it surrendered. Cortés immediately began to rebuild it. He replaced the Aztec religious sites with Christian churches. He also replaced the name of Tenochtitlán. It became Mexico City (right), the capital of what he called New Spain. The Spanish regarded New Spain as an important part of their expanding empire in the New World. Thousands of Spaniards crossed the Atlantic Ocean to live there. Many settled in Mexico City. They intermarried with the native peoples. Their children were called mestizos. Today mestizos make up about 60 percent of Mexico's total population.

Silver was discovered nearby, which added to the wealth that New Spain was sending to Spain. It also prompted many new buildings in Mexico City. They reflected the same architectural styles that were popular in Spain.

Early in the nineteenth century, the Mexicans wanted to become independent. After a ten-year struggle, they threw off Spanish rule in 1821. Mexico City remained the capital. The city saw a variety of rulers. One was Antonio López de Santa Anna. He commanded the Mexican forces at the Battle of the Alamo in Texas. Back home, he ordered the construction of many buildings. They reflected his opinion of how important he was.

The city has experienced explosive growth since the early 1900s, when its population was about 400,000. That was the same size it had been when Cortés arrived. By 1950, the population had risen to about 3 million. By the early 2000s, it was estimated at more than 20 million. One of every five citizens of Mexico lives there.

Mexico City is one of the most important cities in the world. It served as the site of the 1968 Olympic Games. It is dotted with museums and art galleries. Many large companies have their head-quarters there.

The huge lake of Cortés's time is nearly gone. It was drained to allow the city to expand. The drained area beneath the city is unstable. Mexico City suffers considerable damage when earth-quakes strike.

King Charles I of Spain was born in 1500. His parents were Philip the Handsome and Joanna the Mad. Charles became King of Spain in 1516 and ruled for forty years. In 1519, he was also chosen as Holy Roman Emperor and, as such, was called Charles V. He died in 1558.

CHAPTER 5

On to California

Cortés wasn't satisfied with all his new titles. At thirty-seven, he was still a young man. He wanted more adventures.

King Charles didn't entirely trust him. He sent out a royal council to keep an eye on Cortés.

Cortés's wife, Catalina, decided to join him now that he was rich and famous. Her mother and a sister came along. They often complained. Doña Marina was one source of criticism. She was still with Cortés.

The problem was "solved" several months after Catalina's arrival. She was found dead. Many people said Cortés had murdered her, but no one knows whether that is true.

Cortés left Mexico City soon afterward. Cristóbal de Olid, who had been one of his most trusted commanders, had defied Cortés's authority and established a government in Honduras. Cortés could have sent someone else to punish Olid, but he wanted to go himself. Apparently, fighting was more interesting than governing. The expedition lasted two years. Cortés returned triumphant.

He had taken Cuauhtémoc with him to Honduras. He believed that Cuauhtémoc was plotting a rebellion, so Cortés executed him. Some of his men thought Cortés was wrong—he didn't give

Doña Marina was born into royalty but sold into slavery. She was very important to Cortés, both as a translator and companion. Later she married one of his men.

Cuauhtémoc a fair trial. The killing is still important today in Mexico. Cuauhtémoc, as the final Aztec ruler, is a national hero. Cortés is regarded as a villain.

Cortés's enemies had been active while he was gone. They brought numerous legal charges against him. He sailed for Spain in 1528 to defend himself in front of the king. Charles was happy with the gold and the land Cortés had given him, but he still didn't trust Cortés. He didn't want him to become too powerful. He didn't want him to be the governor.

Cortés was allowed to remain captain-general. Charles also gave him a huge estate in Mexico. It was about one-fourth the size of Spain itself. He was the wealthiest man in the new coun-

try. Charles also wanted him to embark on a new adventure. Christopher Columbus had been searching for the mysterious Spice Islands when he discovered the New World. Charles believed there must be a passage from the west coast of New Spain to the Spice Islands. He asked Cortés to find it.

Cortés became a husband again. He married a Spanish noblewoman named Doña Juana Ramírez de Arellano y Zuñiga. She brought him money and eventually six children.

Cortés and his new wife returned to New Spain in 1531. Charles hadn't yet appointed a governor. A committee was in charge of administering the country. Cortés still hoped that Charles would select him. He thought it would be helpful if he could find the route to the Spice Islands. Men under his command discovered what they believed to be a large island west of Mexico. Cortés thought it might be part of the route he was seeking.

Cortés took personal charge. With three ships, he sailed west in 1535. He may have believed that he had discovered the island of Califia, the heroine of a very popular romance. What he had found was Baja California, a desolate and arid wasteland. This very expensive expedition was a failure. No one was interested in a barren strip of land.

In 1537 he received crushing news. Charles had named Don Antonio de Mendoza as governor of New Spain. Cortés swallowed his disappointment. He wanted Mendoza to name him as commander of an ambitious expedition. The object was to discover the legendary Seven Cities of Cibola. These cities were supposedly very rich with gold.

Mendoza had his own man in mind: Don Francisco Vásquez de Coronado. Coronado was about the same age as Cortés had been when he arrived in the New World. Coronado's expedition ranged as far as modern-day Kansas, but he didn't find the cities. That isn't surprising. The Seven Cities of Cibola never existed.

Cortés's restless mind had other plans, but Charles refused to let him lead any more expeditions. In 1540 Cortés returned to Spain to try to change the king's mind. He wasn't successful. Cortés had complained too much. He was boring. Charles paid hardly any attention to him. Cortés became bitter.

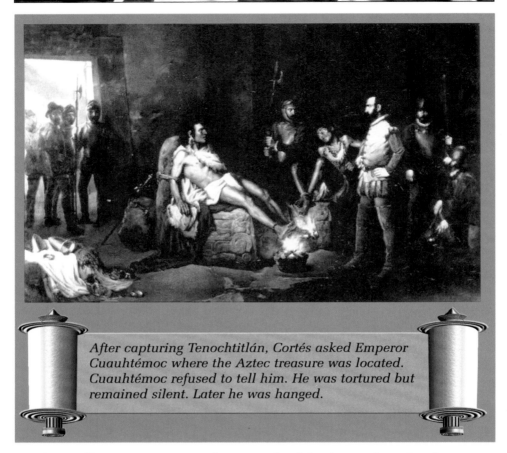

After capturing Tenochtitlán, Cortés asked Emperor Cuauhtémoc where the Aztec treasure was located. Cuauhtémoc refused to tell him. He was tortured but remained silent. Later he was hanged.

According to one story, he saw the king's carriage in the street one day and stepped in front of it. It came to a halt. Charles pretended he didn't recognize Cortés and asked him who he was.

"'I am the man who brought to Your Majesty more kingdoms than your father left you towns,' "[1] Cortés retorted.

The king didn't say a word to Cortés. He ordered his driver to keep going.

Finally even Cortés became discouraged. His health declined. He knew he didn't have much longer to live. He wanted to die in Mexico, the scene of his greatest successes. He was too late. Before he could board a ship, he died in a town near the seaport city of Seville. It was December 2, 1547. He was sixty-two. His descendants eventually brought his remains to Mexico.

By the time of his death, more than a quarter century had elapsed since Cortés had conquered Mexico. Other explorers had become famous, and many people didn't even remember him.

The Mexicans did remember. When the country became independent from Spain in 1821, the victorious generals tried to destroy anything connected with Cortés. He was the primary symbol of Spain, and Mexicans wanted to think of themselves as different from the Spanish. They even tried to find his bones and destroy them. But they couldn't find them. Today, the bones rest in the Hospital de Jesús, which Cortés had founded in 1524. Nearly 500 years later, this hospital was still taking care of patients.

Hospital de Jesús is one of the very few reminders of Cortés in Mexico. In the 1920s and 1930s, famous Mexican painters such as Diego Rivera and David Alfaro Siqueiros painted huge murals that depict Cortés as a brutish, bloodthirsty man. They show him being cruel to the native population.

Several centuries earlier, the Aztecs had given their opinion:

We suffered this bitter fate.
Broken spears lie in the roads;
we have torn our hair in grief.
The houses are roofless now, and their walls
are reddened with blood . . .
We have beat our hands with despair
against the adobe walls
for our inheritance is lost and dead.
The shields of our warriors were its defence,
but they could not save it.[2]

An Aztec witness described his fellow survivors of Tenochtitlán leaving the city after Cortés had conquered it: "The grownups carried the young children on their shoulders. Many of the children were weeping with terror, but one or two laughed and smiled, thinking it great sport to be carried like that by their parents along the road."[3]

They had no way of knowing that they would never see the city again.

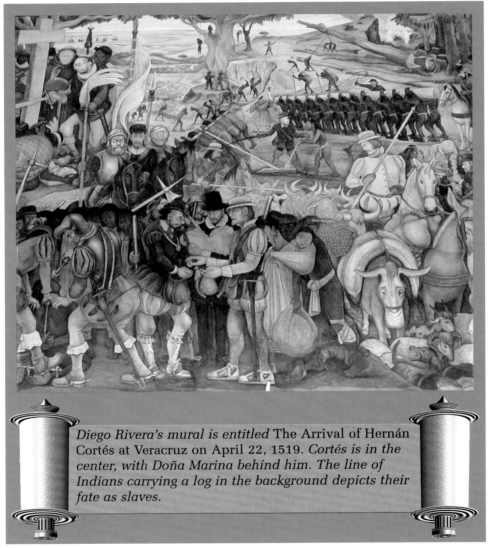

Diego Rivera's mural is entitled The Arrival of Hernán Cortés at Veracruz on April 22, 1519. *Cortés is in the center, with Doña Marina behind him. The line of Indians carrying a log in the background depicts their fate as slaves.*

Some historians defend Cortés. Jon Manchip White points out many of Cortés's positive qualities: courage, leadership, brilliance in conducting military campaigns, founding hospitals, and forming a government that recognized the native people.[4]

Richard Lee Marks adds, "The legacy of Cortés in Mexico . . . was a period of remarkable stability and peace that lasted for about three hundred years. . . . the two phases of living imposed

by Cortés were the factors that kept the peace. . . . Catholic ritual satisfied the people's longing for spiritual answers. Spanish law assured order."[5]

His legacy also was important for the future United States. The country Cortés established played a vital role in the development of the U.S.

Several eighteenth-century expeditions that originated in Mexico established Spanish control over Alta California (the modern-day state of California). These expeditions used the "wasteland" of Baja California as a base.

When Mexico became independent, the new nation invited Americans to move into Texas, the northern part of Mexico. Many Americans took advantage of the invitation. Once they moved in, these Texians wanted to declare independence from Mexico. The result was a war that began in 1835. Mexican president and general Antonio López de Santa Anna defeated the Texians at the Alamo. Soon afterward, he was beaten by Texas leader Sam Houston. Texas became an independent republic.

The Mexican-American War followed a few years later. It ended in 1848 with an overwhelming American victory. The peace treaty gave the United States all or part of seven states: California, Utah, Nevada, Colorado, Arizona, New Mexico, and Wyoming.

Today, Mexico is one of the most important foreign countries to the United States. As its immediate neighbor, it occupies a vital geographic position. Many Mexicans have moved to the United States. They have helped to make Hispanics (as most Spanish-speaking people living in the U.S. are called) the fastest-growing minority in the United States. Hispanic leaders are becoming especially important in American politics.

It is not likely that people will ever completely agree about Cortés. Many people hate him. Others admire him. But there can be no doubt that Hernando Cortés had a profound influence on the history of the Americas.

The Queen of California

Queen Califia appeared in a romance called the *Adventures of Esplandian*. Published in 1510, its author was Garcia Rodríguez de Montalvo. He wrote it on the heels of his tremendously popular *Amadís of Gaul*. This sequel recounts more adventures of the main characters in *Amadís of Gaul*.

According to Montalvo, "There is an island named California . . . which was inhabited by black women, without a single man among them, and that they lived in the manner of Amazons. They were robust of body, with strong and passionate hearts and great virtues. The island itself is one of the wildest in the world on account of the bold and craggy rocks. Their weapons were all made of gold. . . . The island everywhere abounds with gold and precious stones, and upon it no other metal was found. . . . And there ruled over that island of California a queen of majestic proportions, more beautiful than all others, and in the very vigor of her womanhood."[6] The queen's name was Califia.

In the book, a group of Christians in the city of Constantinople is being attacked by a large force of Turks. Califia helps the Turks. Eventually the Christians capture her. She becomes a Christian herself and marries a knight.

Cortés was interested in romance adventures. It is likely that he read the book. Pearls were one of the "precious stones" that Montalvo mentions. Cortés found pearls during his 1535 expedition. He may have believed that he had discovered Califia's island. Most historians believe he named it California in her honor.

An expedition Cortés ordered three years later proved the "island" was actually a peninsula, but the name California remained. Today, the peninsula is known as Baja (lower) California. The body of water between Baja California and Mexico is the Sea of Cortés.

Chapter Notes

Chapter 1   The Night of Sorrows

1. Michael Wood, *Conquistadors* (Berkeley: University of California Press, 2000), p. 76.

2. Miguel Leon-Portilla, editor, *The Broken Spears: The Aztec Account of the Conquest of Mexico*, translated from Nahuatl into Spanish by Angel Maria Garibay K., translated into English by Lysander Kemp (Boston: Beacon Press, 1962), pp. 85–87.

Chapter 2   A Nobody Becomes a Somebody

1. Jon Manchip White, *Cortes and the Downfall of the Aztec Empire* (London: Hamish Hamilton, 1971), p. 21.

2. Richard Lee Marks, *Cortes: The Great Adventurer and the Fate of Aztec Mexico* (New York: Alfred A. Knopf, 1994), p. 38.

3. Miguel Leon-Portilla, editor, *The Broken Spears: The Aztec Account of the Conquest of Mexico*, translated from Nahuatl into Spanish by Angel Maria Garibay K., translated into English by Lysander Kemp (Boston: Beacon Press, 1962), p. ix.

Chapter 3   The Halls of Montezuma

1. Miguel Leon-Portilla, editor, *The Broken Spears: The Aztec Account of the Conquest of Mexico*, translated from Nahuatl into Spanish by Angel Maria Garibay K., translated into English by Lysander Kemp (Boston: Beacon Press, 1962), p. 51.

2. Bernal Díaz del Castillo, *The Discovery and Conquest of Mexico*, translated by A. P. Maudslay (Cambridge, Massachusetts: Da Capo Press, 1996), pp. 190–191.

3. Leon-Portilla, p. 68.

4. Díaz del Castillo, p. 294.

5. Leon-Portilla, p. 76.

Chapter 4   Taking Tenochtitlán

1. Victor Davis Hanson, *Carnage and Culture: Landmark Battles in the Rise of Western Power* (New York: Anchor Books, 2002), p. 185.

2. Bernal Díaz del Castillo, *The Discovery and Conquest of Mexico*, translated by A. P. Maudslay (Cambridge, Massachusetts: Da Capo Press, 1996), pp. 293–294.

3. Hanson, p. 228.

Chapter 5   On to California

1. Jon Manchip White, *Cortes and the Downfall of the Aztec Empire* (London: Hamish Hamilton, 1971), p. 295.

2. Michael Wood, *Conquistadors* (Berkeley: University of California Press, 2000), p. 99.

3. Ibid., p. 98.

4. White, p. 296.

5. Richard Lee Marks, *Cortes: The Great Adventurer and the Fate of Aztec Mexico* (New York: Alfred A. Knopf, 1994), p. 260.

6. The San Francisco African American Historical Cultural Society: Queen Califia Exhibit **http://www.sigidiart.com/Docs/ WandasPicksCalifia.htm**

Chronology

1485 Is born in Medellín in the Spanish province of Extremadura

1499 Begins law studies in Salamanca

1501 Abandons law studies

1504 Arrives in the New World

1511 Goes to Cuba with Diego Velázquez

1514 Marries Catalina Suarez

1519 Begins expedition in Mexico; enters Tenochtitlán

1520 Puts down Narváez; is defeated by the Aztecs on *La Noche Triste*

1521 Returns to Tenochtitlán and captures city

1522 Is named governor of New Spain

1524 Leads expedition to Honduras

1526 Returns to Mexico City; discovers that legal charges have been brought against him

1528 Returns to Spain to defend himself to the king

1529 Is named Marquis of the Valley of Oaxaca

1530 Marries Doña Juana Ramirez de Arellano y Zuñiga, who will bear him six children

1531 Returns to Mexico

1535 Begins expedition to Spice Islands but finds Baja California instead

1540 Returns to Spain

1547 Dies near Seville on December 2

Timeline in History

1431	French heroine Joan of Arc is burned at the stake.
1451	Christopher Columbus is born in Genoa, Italy.
1453	Johannes Gutenberg's Bible is the first book printed using movable type.
1474	William Caxton prints the first book to use the English language.
1492	Columbus lands in the New World.
1497	Portuguese explorer Vasco da Gama sails around the southern tip of Africa.
1502	Columbus begins fourth and final expedition; it includes Honduras and Panama. Montezuma II becomes emperor of Mexico.
1506	Columbus dies.
1513	Ponce de León discovers Florida; Vasco Núñez de Balboa sights the Pacific Ocean.
1516	Charles I is crowned King of Spain.
1519	Ferdinand Magellan begins voyage around the world. King Charles I becomes Holy Roman Emperor Charles V.
1521	Magellan is killed in the Philippine Islands; his men complete the voyage the following year.
1528	Pánfilo de Narváez reaches Florida from Spain.
1531	Francisco Pizarro begins conquest of Peru.
1533	Elizabeth, the future queen of England, is born.
1539	Hernando de Soto lands in Florida.
1540	Francisco Vásquez de Coronado sets out to find the legendary Seven Cities of Cibola.
1547	Miguel de Cervantes, who will write about the fictitious Spanish knight Don Quixote, is born.
1565	Pedro Menéndez de Avilés founds the city of St. Augustine, Florida, the oldest city in the United States.
1588	English ships defeat the Spanish Armada.
1603	Queen Elizabeth dies and is succeeded by her nephew James I.
1607	English establish a colony at Jamestown, Virginia.
1620	English Puritans found Plymouth Colony.

Further Reading

For Young Adults

Calvert, Patricia. *Hernando Cortés: Fortune Favored the Bold*. Tarrytown, New York: Benchmark Books, 2002.

January, Brendan. *Hernán Cortés*. Chicago: Heinemann, 2002.

Koestler-Grack, Rachel A. *Hernándo Cortés and the Fall of the Aztecs*. Broomhall, Pennsylvania: Chelsea House Publishers, 2005.

Molzahn, Arlene Bourgeois. *Hernán Cortés: Conquistador and Explorer*. Berkeley Heights, New Jersey: 2003.

Works Consulted

Díaz del Castillo, Bernal. *The Discovery and Conquest of Mexico*. Translated by A. P. Maudslay. Cambridge, Massachusetts: Da Capo Press, 1996.

Hanson, Victor Davis. *Carnage and Culture: Landmark Battles in the Rise of Western Power*. New York: Anchor Books, 2002.

Leon-Portilla, Miguel (editor). *The Broken Spears: The Aztec Account of the Conquest of Mexico*. Translated from Nahuatl into Spanish by Angel Maria Garibay K. Translated into English by Lysander Kemp. Boston: Beacon Press, 1962.

Marks, Richard Lee. *Cortés: The Great Adventurer and the Fate of Aztec Mexico*. New York: Alfred A. Knopf, 1994.

White, Jon Manchip. *Cortés and the Downfall of the Aztec Empire*. London: Hamish Hamilton, 1971.

Wood, Michael. *Conquistadors*. Berkeley: University of California Press, 2000.

On the Internet

San Francisco Bay View—Wanda's Picks: Queen Califia Exhibit
http://www.sigidiart.com/Docs/WandasPicksCalifia.htm

Palfrey, Dale Hoyte. Mexico History—The Spanish Conquest (1519–1521)
http://www.mexconnect.com/mex_/travel/dpalfrey/dpconquest.html

Hooker, Richard. Civilizations in America: The Mayas.
http://wsu.edu/~dee/CIVAMRCA/MAYAS.HTM

A Brief History of Chocolate
http://www.godiva.com/about/history.aspx

The History of Chocolate
http://www.whetstonechocolates.com/html/history.htm

CIA—The World Factbook—Mexico
https://www.cia.gov/cia/publications/factbook/print/mx.html

Economist.com—Cities Guide: Mexico City
http://www.economist.com/cities/findStory.cfm?city_id=MEX&folder=Facts-History

Glossary

adobe (uh-DOH-bee)
Building material made of mud and straw.

Amazons (AA-muh-zons)
Powerful female warriors who are featured in Greek mythology; they are especially famous for their skill with bows and arrows.

besieged (bee-SEEJD)
Surrounded by enemies.

causeway (COZ-way)
A narrow roadway that crosses a body of water and is elevated several feet above water level.

contingents (kun-TIN-juntz)
Small detachments from a much larger group.

crossbows (CROSS-bohz)
Small, powerful bows mounted on thick strips of wood; they fire darts under a great deal of pressure.

emissary (EH-muh-sair-ee)
A representative of another person.

harquebus (HARK-bus)
A primitive form of the rifle.

hostage (HOS-tij)
A person captured and held prisoner to use as a trade for something the captor demands.

masonry (MAY-sun-ree)
Stout building materials such as bricks or stones.

mythical (MIH-thuh-kul)
Something that is legendary or imaginary rather than historical.

provocation (prah-vuh-KAY-shun)
Something that deliberately stirs up action.

ravenous (RAA-vuh-nuss)
Very eager for something, especially food.

Texian (TEK-see-in)
A person who lived in Texas before it became a state.

Index